SLABS OF THE SUNBURNT WEST

BY 1 304

CARL SANDBURG

AUTHOR OF "SMOKE AND STEEL," "CHICAGO POEMS,"
"CORNHUSKERS"

NEW YORK
HARCOURT, BRACE AND COMPANY

PRINTED IN THE U. S. A. BY
THE QUINN & BODEN COMPANY
RAHWAY, N. J

TO
HELGA

Acknowledgments are due to the editors of *Poetry* (Chicago), *The New Republic, The Bookman, The Century, Harper's Monthly, The Measure, The Dial, Vanity Fair, The Nation, The Liberator, The Freeman,* in whose pages some of the writings herein have appeared.

CONTENTS

SLABS OF THE SUNBURNT WEST

THE WINDY CITY

I

THE lean hands of wagon men
put out pointing fingers here,
picked this crossway, put it on a map,
set up their sawbucks, fixed their shotguns,
found a hitching place for the pony express,
made a hitching place for the iron horse,
the one-eyed horse with the fire-spit head,
found a homelike spot and said, " Make a home,"
saw this corner with a mesh of rails, shuttling
    people, shunting cars, shaping the junk of
    the earth to a new city.

The hands of men took hold and tugged
And the breaths of men went into the junk
And the junk stood up into skyscrapers and asked:
Who am I? Am I a city? And if I am what is my name?
And once while the time whistles blew and blew again
The men answered: Long ago we gave you a name,
Long ago we laughed and said: You? Your name is
    Chicago.

Early the red men gave a name to a river,
    the place of the skunk,
    the river of the wild onion smell,
    Shee-caw-go.

Out of the payday songs of steam shovels,
Out of the wages of structural iron rivets,
The living lighted skyscrapers tell it now as a name,
Tell it across miles of sea blue water, gray blue land:
I am Chicago, I am a name given out by the breaths of
     working men, laughing men, a child, a belonging.

So between the Great Lakes,
The Grand De Tour, and the Grand Prairie,
The living lighted skyscrapers stand,
Spotting the blue dusk with checkers of yellow,
    streamers of smoke and silver,
    parallelograms of night-gray watchmen,
Singing a soft moaning song: I am a child, a belonging.

2

How should the wind songs of a windy city go?
Singing in a high wind the dirty chatter gets blown
    away on the wind—the clean shovel,
         the clean pickax,
         lasts.

It is easy for a child to get breakfast and pack off
    to school with a pair of roller skates,
    buns for lunch, and a geography.
Riding through a tunnel under a river running backward,
    to school to listen . . . how the Pottawattamies . . .
    and the Blackhawks . . . ran on moccasins . . .
    between Kaskaskia, Peoria, Kankakee, and Chicago.

It is easy to sit listening to a boy babbling
    of the Pottawattamie moccasins in Illinois,
    how now the roofs and smokestacks cover miles
    where the deerfoot left its writing
    and the foxpaw put its initials
    in the snow . . . for the early moccasins . . . to
        read.

It is easy for the respectable taxpayers to sit in the
    street cars and read the papers, faces of burglars,
    the prison escapes, the hunger strikes, the cost of
    living, the price of dying, the shop gate battles of
    strikers and strikebreakers, the strikers killing
    scabs and the police killing strikers—the strongest,
    the strongest, always the strongest.

It is easy to listen to the haberdasher customers hand
    each other their easy chatter—it is easy to die
    alive—to register a living thumbprint and be dead
    from the neck up.
And there are sidewalks polished with the footfalls of
    undertakers' stiffs, greased mannikins, wearing up-to-
    the-minute sox, lifting heels across doorsills,
    shoving their faces ahead of them—dead from the
    neck up—proud of their sox—their sox are the last
    word—dead from the neck up—it is easy.

3

Lash yourself to the bastion of a bridge
and listen while the black cataracts of people go by,
        baggage, bundles, balloons,
      listen while they jazz the classics:

   " Since when did you kiss yourself in
     And who do you think you are?
     Come across, kick in, loosen up.
     Where do you get that chatter? "

   " Beat up the short change artists.
     They never did nothin' for you.
     How do you get that way?
     Tell me and I'll tell the world.
     I'll say so, I'll say it is."

   " You're trying to crab my act.
     You poor fish, you mackerel,
     You ain't got the sense God
     Gave an oyster—it's raining—
     What you want is an umbrella."

     " Hush baby—
   I don't know a thing.
   I don't know a thing.
     Hush baby."

     " Hush baby,
   It ain't how old you are,

It's how old you look.
It ain't what you got,
It's what you can get away with."

" Bring home the bacon.
Put it over, shoot it across.
Send 'em to the cleaners.
What we want is results, re-sults
And damn the consequences.
Sh . . . sh. . . .
You can fix anything
If you got the right fixers."

" Kid each other, you cheap skates.
Tell each other you're all to the mustard—
You're the gravy."

" Tell 'em, honey.
Ain't it the truth, sweetheart?
Watch your step.
You said it.
You said a mouthful.
We're all a lot of damn fourflushers."

" Hush baby!
Shoot it,
Shoot it all!
Coo coo, coo coo "—
This is one song of Chicago.

4

It is easy to come here a stranger and show the whole
   works, write a book, fix it all up—it is easy to come
   and go away a muddle-headed pig, a bum and a
   bag of wind.

Go to it and remember this city fished from its
   depths a text: " independent as a hog on ice."
Venice is a dream of soft waters, Vienna and Bagdad
   recollections of dark spears and wild turbans; Paris
   is a thought in Monet gray on scabbards, fabrics,
   façades; London is a fact in a fog filled with the
   moaning of transatlantic whistles; Berlin sits amid
   white scrubbed quadrangles and torn arithmetics and
   testaments; Moscow brandishes a flag and repeats a
   dance figure of a man who walks like a bear.
Chicago fished from its depths a text: Independent
   as a hog on ice.

5

Forgive us if the monotonous houses go mile on mile
Along monotonous streets out to the prairies—
If the faces of the houses mumble hard words
At the streets—and the street voices only say:
" Dust and a bitter wind shall come."

Forgive us if the lumber porches and doorsteps
Snarl at each other—
And the brick chimneys cough in a close-up of
Each other's faces—
And the ramshackle stairways watch each other
As thieves watch—
And dooryard lilacs near a malleable iron works
Long ago languished
In a short whispering purple.

And if the alley ash cans
Tell the garbage wagon drivers
The children play the alley is Heaven
And the streets of Heaven shine
With a grand dazzle of stones of gold
And there are no policemen in Heaven—
Let the rag-tags have it their way.

And if the geraniums
In the tin cans of the window sills
Ask questions not worth answering—
And if a boy and a girl hunt the sun
With a sieve for sifting smoke—
Let it pass—let the answer be—
" Dust and a bitter wind shall come."

Forgive us if the jazz timebeats
Of these clumsy mass shadows
Moan in saxophone undertones,

And the footsteps of the jungle,
The fang cry, the rip claw hiss,
The sneak-up and the still watch,
The slant of the slit eyes waiting—
If these bother respectable people
        with the right crimp in their napkins
        reading breakfast menu cards—
        forgive us—let it pass—let be.

If cripples sit on their stumps
And joke with the newsies bawling,
" Many lives lost! many lives lost!
Ter-ri-ble ac-ci-dent! many lives lost! "—
If again twelve men let a woman go,
" He done me wrong; I shot him "—
Or the blood of a child's head
Spatters on the hub of a motor truck—
Or a 44-gat cracks and lets the skylights
Into one more bank messenger—
Or if boys steal coal in a railroad yard
And run with humped gunnysacks
While a bull picks off one of the kids
And the kid wriggles with an ear in cinders
And a mother comes to carry home
A bundle, a limp bundle,
To have his face washed, for the last time,
Forgive us if it happens—and happens again—
And happens again.

        Forgive the jazz timebeat
        of clumsy mass shadows,

footsteps of the jungle,
the fang cry, the rip claw hiss,
the slant of the slit eyes waiting.

Forgive us if we work so hard
And the muscles bunch clumsy on us
And we never know why we work so hard—
If the big houses with little families
And the little houses with big families
Sneer at each other's bars of misunderstanding;
Pity us when we shackle and kill each other
And believe at first we understand
And later say we wonder why.

Take home the monotonous patter
Of the elevated railroad guard in the rush hours:
" Watch your step. Watch your step. Watch your step."
Or write on a pocket pad what a pauper said
To a patch of purple asters at a whitewashed wall:
" Let every man be his own Jesus—that's enough."

6

The wheelbarrows grin, the shovels and the mortar
    hoist an exploit.
The stone shanks of the Monadnock, the Transportation,
    the People's Gas Building, stand up and scrape
    at the sky.
The wheelbarrows sing, the bevels and the blue prints
    whisper.

The library building named after Crerar, naked
    as a stock farm silo, light as a single eagle
    feather, stripped like an airplane propeller,
    takes a path up.
Two cool new rivets say, " Maybe it is morning,"
    " God knows."

Put the city up; tear the city down;
    put it up again; let us find a city.
Let us remember the little violet-eyed
    man who gave all, praying, " Dig and
    dream, dream and hammer, till your
    city comes."

Every day the people sleep and the city dies;
    every day the people shake loose, awake and
    build the city again.

The city is a tool chest opened every day,
    a time clock punched every morning,
    a shop door, bunkers and overalls
    counting every day.

The city is a balloon and a bubble plaything
    shot to the sky every evening, whistled in
    a ragtime jig down the sunset.

The city is made, forgotten, and made again,
    trucks hauling it away haul it back
    steered by drivers whistling ragtime
    against the sunsets.

Every day the people get up and carry the city,
    carry the bunkers and balloons of the city,
    lift it and put it down.

    " I will die as many times
      as you make me over again,
      says the city to the people,
" I am the woman, the home, the family,
I get breakfast and pay the rent;
I telephone the doctor, the milkman, the undertaker;
    I fix the streets
    for your first and your last ride—
" Come clean with me, come clean or dirty,
I am stone and steel of your sleeping numbers;
    I remember all you forget.
    I will die as many times
    as you make me over again."

Under the foundations,
Over the roofs,
The bevels and the blue prints talk it over.
The wind of the lake shore waits and wanders.
The heave of the shore wind hunches the sand piles.
The winkers of the morning stars count out cities
And forget the numbers.

7

At the white clock-tower
lighted in night purples
over the boulevard link bridge
only the blind get by without acknowledgments.

The passers-by, factory punch-clock numbers,
 hotel girls out for the air, teameoes,
 coal passers, taxi drivers, window washers,
 paperhangers, floorwalkers, bill collectors,
 burglar alarm salesmen, massage students,
 manicure girls, chiropodists, bath rubbers,
 booze runners, hat cleaners, armhole basters,
 delicatessen clerks, shovel stiffs, work plugs—
They all pass over the bridge, they all look up
 at the white clock-tower
 lighted in night purples
 over the boulevard link bridge—
 And sometimes one says, " Well, we hand it to 'em."

Mention proud things, catalogue them.
The jack-knife bridge opening, the ore boats,
 the wheat barges passing through.
Three overland trains arriving the same hour,
 one from Memphis and the cotton belt,
 one from Omaha and the corn belt,
 one from Duluth, the lumberjack and the iron range.
Mention a carload of shorthorns taken off the valleys
 of Wyoming last week, arriving yesterday, knocked in
 the head, stripped, quartered, hung in ice boxes
 to-day, mention the daily melodrama of this hum-
 drum, rhythms of heads, hides, heels, hoofs hung up.

8

It is wisdom to think the people are the city.
It is wisdom to think the city would fall to pieces
 and die and be dust in the wind.

If the people of the city all move away and leave no
    people at all to watch and keep the city.
It is wisdom to think no city stood here at all until
    the working men, the laughing men, came.
It is wisdom to think to-morrow new working men, new
    laughing men, may come and put up a new city—
Living lighted skyscrapers and a night lingo of lanterns
    testify to-morrow shall have its own say-so.

9

Night gathers itself into a ball of dark yarn.
Night loosens the ball and it spreads.
The lookouts from the shores of Lake Michigan
    find night follows day, and ping! ping! across
    sheet gray the boat lights put their signals.
Night lets the dark yarn unravel, Night speaks and
    the yarns change to fog and blue strands.

The lookouts turn to the city.
The canyons swarm with red sand lights
    of the sunset.
The atoms drop and sift, blues cross over,
    yellows plunge.
Mixed light shafts stack their bayonets,
    pledge with crossed handles.
So, when the canyons swarm, it is then the
    lookouts speak
Of the high spots over a street . . . mountain language
Of skyscrapers in dusk, the Railway Exchange,
The People's Gas, the Monadnock, the Transportation,
Gone to the gloaming.

The river turns in a half circle.
The Goose Island bridges curve
    over the river curve.
    Then the river panorama
    performs for the bridge,
    dots . . . lights . . . dots . . . lights,
    sixes and sevens of dots and lights,
    a lingo of lanterns and searchlights,
    circling sprays of gray and yellow.

10

A man came as a witness saying:
" I listened to the Great Lakes
And I listened to the Grand Prairie,
And they had little to say to each other,
A whisper or so in a thousand years.
' Some of the cities are big,' said one.
' And some not so big,' said another.
' And sometimes the cities are all gone,'
Said a black knob bluff to a light green sea."

Winds of the Windy City, come out of the prairie,
    all the way from Medicine Hat.
Come out of the inland sea blue water, come where
    they nickname a city for you.

Corn wind in the fall, come off the black lands,
    come off the whisper of the silk hangers,
    the lap of the flat spear leaves.

Blue water wind in summer, come off the blue miles
    of lake, carry your inland sea blue fingers,
    carry us cool, carry your blue to our homes.

White spring winds, come off the bag wool clouds,
    come off the running melted snow, come white
    as the arms of snow-born children.

Gray fighting winter winds, come along on the tear-
    ing blizzard tails, the snouts of the hungry
    hunting storms, come fighting gray in winter.

Winds of the Windy City,
Winds of corn and sea blue,
Spring wind white and fighting winter gray,
Come home here—they nickname a city for you.

The wind of the lake shore waits and wanders.
The heave of the shore wind hunches the sand piles.
The winkers of the morning stars count out cities
And forget the numbers.

WASHINGTON MONUMENT BY NIGHT

1

THE stone goes straight.
A lean swimmer dives into night sky,
Into half-moon mist.

2

Two trees are coal black.
This is a great white ghost between.
It is cool to look at.
Strong men, strong women, come here.

3

Eight years is a long time
To be fighting all the time.

4

The republic is a dream.
Nothing happens unless first a dream.

5

The wind bit hard at Valley Forge one Christmas.
Soldiers tied rags on their feet.

Red footprints wrote on the snow . . .
. . . and stone shoots into stars here
. . . into half-moon mist to-night.

6

Tongues wrangled dark at a man.
He buttoned his overcoat and stood alone.
In a snowstorm, red hollyberries, thoughts,
    he stood alone.

7

Women said: He is lonely
. . . fighting . . . fighting . . . eight years . . .

8

The name of an iron man goes over the world.
It takes a long time to forget an iron man.

9

. . .   .
. . .   .

AND SO TO-DAY

AND so to-day—they lay him away—
the boy nobody knows the name of—
the buck private—the unknown soldier—
the doughboy who dug under and died
when they told him to—that's him.

Down Pennsylvania Avenue to-day the riders go,
men and boys riding horses, roses in their teeth,
stems of roses, rose leaf stalks, rose dark leaves—
the line of the green ends in a red rose flash.

Skeleton men and boys riding skeleton horses,
the rib bones shine, the rib bones curve,
shine with savage, elegant curves—
a jawbone runs with a long white slant,
a skull dome runs with a long white arch,
bone triangles click and rattle,
elbows, ankles, white line slants—
shining in the sun, past the White House,
past the Treasury Building, Army and Navy Buildings,
on to the mystic white Capitol Dome—
so they go down Pennsylvania Avenue to-day,
skeleton men and boys riding skeleton horses,
stems of roses in their teeth,

rose dark leaves at their white jaw slants—
and a horse laugh question nickers and whinnies,
moans with a whistle out of horse head teeth:
why? who? where?

  (" The big fish—eat the little fish—
    the little fish—eat the shrimps—
    and the shrimps—eat mud."—
    said a cadaverous man—with a black umbrella—
    spotted with white polka dots—with a missing
    ear—with a missing foot and arms—
    with a missing sheath of muscles
    singing to the silver sashes of the sun.)

And so to-day—they lay him away—
the boy nobody knows the name of—
the buck private—the unknown soldier—
the doughboy who dug under and died
when they told him to—that's him.

If he picked himself and said, " I am ready to die,"
if he gave his name and said, " My country, take me,"
then the baskets of roses to-day are for the Boy,
the flowers, the songs, the steamboat whistles,
the proclamations of the honorable orators,
they are all for the Boy—that's him.

If the government of the Republic picked him saying,
" You are wanted, your country takes you "—
if the Republic put a stethoscope to his heart
and looked at his teeth and tested his eyes and said,

" You are a citizen of the Republic and a sound animal
in all parts and functions—the Republic takes you "—
then to-day the baskets of flowers are all for the Republic,
the roses, the songs, the steamboat whistles,
the proclamations of the honorable orators—
they are all for the Republic.

And so to-day—they lay him away—
and an understanding goes—his long sleep shall be
under arms and arches near the Capitol Dome—
there is an authorization—he shall have tomb com-
    panions—
the martyred presidents of the Republic—
the buck private—the unknown soldier—that's him.

The man who was war commander of the armies of the
    Republic
rides down Pennsylvania Avenue—
The man who is peace commander of the armies of the
    Republic
rides down Pennsylvania Avenue—
for the sake of the Boy, for the sake of the Republic.

(And the hoofs of the skeleton horses
all drum soft on the asphalt footing—
so soft is the drumming, so soft the roll call
of the grinning sergeants calling the roll call—
so soft is it all—a camera man murmurs, " Moon-
    shine.")

Look—who salutes the coffin—
lays a wreath of remembrance
on the box where a buck private
sleeps a clean dry sleep at last—
look—it is the highest ranking general
of the officers of the armies of the Republic.

(Among pigeon corners of the Congressional Library
—they file documents quietly, casually, all in a day's
work—this human document, the buck private
nobody knows the name of—they file away in granite and steel—with music and roses, salutes, proclamations of the honorable orators.)

Across the country, between two ocean shore lines,
where cities cling to rail and water routes,
there people and horses stop in their foot tracks,
cars and wagons stop in their wheel tracks—
faces at street crossings shine with a silence
of eggs laid in a row on a pantry shelf—
among the ways and paths of the flow of the Republic
faces come to a standstill, sixty clockticks count—
in the name of the Boy, in the name of the Republic.

(A million faces a thousand miles from Pennsylvania
Avenue stay frozen with a look, a clocktick, a
moment—skeleton riders on skeleton horses—the
nickering high horse laugh, the whinny and the
howl up Pennsylvania Avenue: who? why? where?)

(So people far from the asphalt footing of Pennsylvania Avenue look, wonder, mumble—the riding
white-jaw phantoms ride hi-eeee, hi-eeee, hi-yi, hi-yi,
hi-eeee—the proclamations of the honorable orators
mix with the top-sergeants whistling the roll call.)

If when the clockticks counted sixty,
when the heartbeats of the Republic
came to a stop for a minute,
if the Boy had happened to sit up,
happening to sit up as Lazarus sat up, in the story,
then the first shivering language to drip off his mouth
might have come as, " Thank God," or " Am I
     dreaming? "
or " What the hell " or " When do we eat? "
or " Kill 'em, kill 'em, the . . ."
or " Was that . . . a rat . . . ran over my face? "
or " For Christ's sake, gimme water, gimme water,"
or " Blub blub, bloo bloo. . . . . . ."
or any bubbles of shell shock gibberish
from the gashes of No Man's Land.

Maybe some buddy knows,
some sister, mother, sweetheart,
maybe some girl who sat with him once
when a two-horn silver moon
slid on the peak of a house-roof gable,
and promises lived in the air of the night,
when the air was filled with promises,
when any little slip-shoe lovey
could pick a promise out of the air.

" Feed it to 'em,
      they lap it up,
      bull . . . bull . . . bull,"
Said a movie news reel camera man,
Said a Washington newspaper correspondent,
Said a baggage handler lugging a trunk,
Said a two-a-day vaudeville juggler,
Said a hanky-pank selling jumping-jacks.
" Hokum—they lap it up," said the bunch.

And a tall scar-face ball player,
Played out as a ball player,
Made a speech of his own for the hero boy,
Sent an earful of his own to the dead buck private:
      " It's all safe now, buddy,
      Safe when you say yes,
      Safe for the yes-men."

He was a tall scar-face battler
With his face in a newspaper
Reading want ads, reading jokes,
Reading love, murder, politics,
Jumping from jokes back to the want ads,
Reading the want ads first and last,
The letters of the word JOB, " J-O-B,"
Burnt like a shot of bootleg booze
In the bones of his head—
In the wish of his scar-face eyes.

The honorable orators,
Always the honorable orators,
Buttoning the buttons on their prinz alberts,
Pronouncing the syllables " sac-ri-fice,"
Juggling those bitter salt-soaked syllables—
Do they ever gag with hot ashes in their mouths?
Do their tongues ever shrivel with a pain of fire
Across those simple syllables " sac-ri-fice " ?

(There was one orator people far off saw.
He had on a gunnysack shirt over his bones,
And he lifted an elbow socket over his head,
And he lifted a skinny signal finger.
And he had nothing to say, nothing easy—
He mentioned ten million men, mentioned them as having
        gone west, mentioned them as shoving up the daisies.
We could write it all on a postage stamp, what he said.
He said it and quit and faded away,
A gunnysack shirt on his bones.)

        Stars of the night sky,
        did you see that phantom fadeout,
        did you see those phantom riders,
        skeleton riders on skeleton horses,
        stems of roses in their teeth,
        rose leaves red on white-jaw slants,
        grinning along on Pennsylvania Avenue,
        the top-sergeants calling roll calls—
        did their horses nicker a horse laugh?
        did the ghosts of the boney battalions
        move out and on, up the Potomac, over on the Ohio,

and out to the Mississippi, the Missouri, the Red
  River,
and down to the Rio Grande, and on to the Yazoo,
over to the Chattahoochee and up to the Rappa-
  hannock?
did you see 'em, stars of the night sky?

And so to-day—they lay him away—
the boy nobody knows the name of—
they lay him away in granite and steel—
with music and roses—under a flag—
under a sky of promises.

BLACK HORIZONS

BLACK horizons, come up.
Black horizons, kiss me.
That is all; so many lies; killing so cheap;
babies so cheap; blood, people, so cheap; and
land high, land dear; a speck of the earth
costs; a suck at the tit of Mother Dirt so
clean and strong, it costs; fences, papers,
sheriffs; fences, laws, guns; and so many
stars and so few hours to dream; such a big
song and so little a footing to stand and
sing; take a look; wars to come; red rivers
to cross.
Black horizons, come up.
Black horizons, kiss me.

SEA   SLANT

On up the sea slant,
On up the horizon,
This ship limps.

The bone of her nose fog-gray,
The heart of her sea-strong,
She came a long way,
She goes a long way.

On up the horizon,
On up the sea-slant,
She limps sea-strong, fog-gray.

She is a green-lit night gray.
She comes and goes in sea fog.
Up the horizon slant she limps.

UPSTREAM

THE strong men keep coming on.
They go down shot, hanged, sick,
    broken.
They live on fighting, singing,
    lucky as plungers.
The strong mothers pulling them
    on . .
The strong mothers pulling them
    from a dark sea, a great prairie,
    a long mountain.
Call hallelujah, call amen, call
    deep thanks.
The strong men keep coming on.

FOUR STEICHEN PRINTS

THE earth, the rock and the oil of the earth, the slippery frozen places of the earth, these are for homes of rainbow bubbles, curves of the circles of a bubble, curves of the arcs of the rainbow prisms—between sun and rock they lift to the sun their foam feather and go.

. .

Throw your neck back, throw it back till the neck muscles shine at the sun, till the falling hair at the scalp is a black cry, till limbs and knee bones form an altar, and a girl's torso over the fire-rock torso shouts hi yi, hi yee, hallelujah.

. .

Goat girl caught in the brambles, deerfoot or fox-head, ankles and hair of feeders of the wind, let all the covering burn, let all stopping a naked plunger from plunging naked, let it all burn in this wind fire, let the fire have it in a fast crunch and a flash.

. .

They threw you into a pot of thorns with a wreath in your hair and bunches of grapes over your head—your hard little buttocks in the thorns—then the black eyes, the white teeth, the nameless muscular flair of you, rippled and twisted in sliding rising scales of laughter; the earth never had a gladder friend; pigs, goats, deer, tawny tough-haired jaguars might understand you.

FINS

PLOW over bars of sea plowing,
the moon by moon work of the sea,
the plowing, sand and rock, must
be done.

Ride over, ride over bars of sea riding,
the sun and the blue riding of the sea—
sit in the saddles and say it, sea riders.

Slant up and go, silver breakers; mix
the high howls of your dancing; shoot
your laugh of rainbow foam tops.

Foam wings, fly; pick the comers, the fin pink,
the belly green, the blue rain sparks, the
white wave spit—fly, you foam wings.

The men of the sea are gone to work; the women
of the sea are off buying new hats, combs, clocks;
it is rust and gold on the roofs of the sea.

BEAT, OLD HEART

BEAT, old heart, these are the old bars
All strugglers have beat against.
Beat on these bars like the old sea
Beats on the rocks and beaches.
Beat here like the old winter winds
Beat on the prairies and timbers.
Old grizzlies, eagles, buffalo,
Their paws and beaks register this.
Their hides and heads say it with scars.

MOON RIDERS

1

WHAT have I saved out of a morning?
The earliest of the morning came with moon-mist
And the travel of a moon-spilt purple;
  Bars, horseshoes, Texas longhorns,
  Linked in night silver,
  Linked under leaves in moonlit silver,
  Linked in rags and patches
  Out of the ice houses of the morning moon.
  Yes, this was the earliest—
  Before the cowpunchers on the eastern rims
  Began riding into the sun,
  Riding the roan mustangs of morning,
  Roping the mavericks after the latest stars.
  What have I saved out of a morning?
  Was there a child face I saw once
  Smiling up a stairway of the morning moon?

2

" It is time for work," said a man in the morning.
He opened the faces of the clocks, saw their works,
Saw the wheels oiled and fitted, running smooth.
" It is time to begin a day's work," he said again,
Watching a bull-finch hop on the rain-worn boards

Of a beaten fence counting its bitter winters.
The slinging feet of the bull-finch and the flash
Of its flying feathers as it flipped away
Took his eyes away from the clocks, his flying eyes.
He walked over, stood in front of the clocks again
And said, " I'm sorry; I apologize forty ways."

3

  The morning paper lay bundled
  Like a spear in a museum
  Across the broken sleeping room
  Of a moon-sheet spider.
The spinning work of the morning spider's feet
Left off where the morning paper's pages lay
In the shine of the web in the summer dew grass.
The man opened the morning paper, saw the first page,
The back page, the inside pages, the editorials,
Saw the world go by, eating, stealing, fighting,
Saw the headlines, date lines, funnies, ads,
The marching movies of the workmen going to work,
  the workmen striking,
The workmen asking jobs—five million pairs of eyes look
  for a boss and say, " Take *me*,"
People eating with too much to eat, people eating with
  nothing in sight to eat to-morrow, eating as though
  eating belongs where people belong.

" Hustle, you hustlers, while the hustling's good,"
Said the man, turning the morning paper's pages,
Turning among headlines, date lines, funnies, ads.

" Hustlers carrying the banner," said the man
Dropping the paper and beginning to hunt the city,
Hunting the alleys, boulevards, back-door by-ways,
Hunting till he found a blind horse dying alone,
Telling the horse, " Two legs or four legs—it's all the
    same with a work plug."

A hayfield mist of evening saw him
Watching moon riders lose the moon
For new shooting stars—he asked,
" Christ, what have I saved out of a morning? "
He called up a stairway of the morning moon
And he remembered a child face smiling up that same
    stairway.

AT THE GATES OF TOMBS

CIVILIZATIONS are set up and knocked down
the same as pins in a bowling alley.

Civilizations get into the garbage wagons
and are hauled away the same as potato
peelings or any pot scrapings.

Civilizations, all the work of the artists,
inventors, dreamers of work and genius,
go to the dumps one by one.

Be silent about it; since at the gates of tombs
silence is a gift, be silent; since at the epitaphs
written in the air, since at the swan songs hung in
the air, silence is a gift, be silent; forget it.

If any fool, babbler, gabby mouth, stand up and say:
Let us make a civilization where the sacred and
beautiful things of toil and genius shall last—

If any such noisy gazook stands up and makes himself
heard—put him out—tie a can on him—lock him up
in Leavenworth—shackle him in the Atlanta hoosegow
—let him eat from the tin dishes at Sing Sing—
slew him in as a lifer at San Quentin.

It is the law; as a civilization dies and goes down
to eat ashes along with all other dead civilizations
—it is the law all dirty wild dreamers die first—
gag 'em, lock 'em up, get 'em bumped off.

And since at the gates of tombs silence is a gift,
be silent about it, yes, be silent—forget it.

HAZARDOUS OCCUPATIONS

JUGGLERS keep six bottles in the air.
Club swingers toss up six and eight.
The knife throwers miss each other's
      ears by a hair and the steel quivers
      in the target wood.
The trapeze battlers do a back-and-forth
      high in the air with a girl's feet
      and ankles upside down.
So they earn a living—till they miss
      once, twice, even three times.
So they live on hate and love as gypsies
      live in satin skins and shiny eyes.
In their graves do the elbows jostle once
      in a blue moon—and wriggle to throw
      a kiss answering a dreamed-of applause?
Do the bones repeat: It's a *good* act—
      we got a *good* hand. . . . ?

PROPS

1

ROLL open this rug; a minx is
in it; see her toe wiggling;
roll open the rug; she is a
runaway; or somebody is trying
to steal her; here she is;
here's your minx; how can we
have a play unless we have
this minx?

2

The child goes out in the storm
stage thunder; " erring daughter,
never darken this door-sill again ";
the tender parents speak their curse;
the child puts a few knick-knacks in
a handkerchief; and the child goes;
the door closes and the child goes;
she is out now, in the storm on the
stage, out forever; snow, you son-of-a-gun,
snow, turn on the snow.

GYPSY MOTHER

In a hole-in-a-wall on Halsted Street sits a gypsy
    woman,
In a garish gas-lit rendezvous, in a humpback higgling
    hole-in-a-wall.

The left hand is a tattler; stars and oaths and alphabets
Commit themselves and tell happenings gone, happenings
    to come, pathways of honest people, hypocrites.

" Long pointed fingers mean imagination; a star on the
    third finger says a black shadow walks near."
Cross the gypsy's hand with fifty cents and she takes
    your left hand and reads how you shall be happy in
    love, or not, and whether you die rich, or not.
Signs outside the hole-in-a-wall say so, misspell the
    promises, scrawl the superior gypsy mysteries.

A red shawl on her shoulders falls with a fringe hem to
    a green skirt;
Chains of yellow beads sweep from her neck to her tawny
    hands.
Fifty springtimes must have kissed her mouth holding a
    calabash pipe.
She pulls slow contemplative puffs of smoke; she is a
    shape for ghosts of contemplation to sit around and

ask why something cheap as happiness is here and
more besides, chapped lips, rough eyes, red shawl.
She is thinking about somebody and something the same
as Whistler's mother sat and thought about somebody and something.

In a hole-in-a-wall on Halsted Street are stars, oaths,
alphabets.

GOLD MUD

(For R. F.)

THE pot of gold at the rainbow end
    is a pot of mud, gold mud,
    slippery shining mud.

Pour it on your hair and you will
    have a golden hair.
Pour it on your cat and you will
    have a golden cat.
Pour it on your clock and you will
    have a golden clock.

Pour it on a dead man's thumb and
    you will have a golden thumb
    to bring you bad dreams.
Pour it on a dead woman's ear and
    you will have a golden ear
    to tell hard luck stories to.
Pour it on a horse chestnut and you
    will have a golden buckeye
    changing your luck.

Pour it in the shape of a holy cross,
    fasten it on my shirt for me to wear
    and I will have a keepsake.
I will touch it and say a prayer for you.

CROSSING THE PACES

THE Sioux sat around their wigwam fires
in winter with some papooses hung up
and some laid down.
And the Sioux had a saying, " Love grows
like hair on a black bear's skin."

The Arabians spill this: The first gray
hair is a challenge of death.
A Polish blacksmith: A good blacksmith is not afraid of smoke.
And a Scandinavian warns: The world was born
in fire and he who is fire himself will be
at home anywhere on earth.
So a stranger told his children: You are
strangers—and warned them:

Bob your hair; or let it grow long;
Be a company, a party, a picnic;
Be alone, a nut, a potato, an orange blossom,
     a keg of nails; if you get lost try a
     want ad; if night comes try a long sleep.

COUPLES

Six miasmic women in green
danced an absinthe dance
hissing oaths of laughter
at six men they cheated.

Six miasmic men did the same
for six women they cheated.

It was a stand-off
in oaths of laughter hissed;

The dirt is hard where they danced.
The pads of their feet made a floor.

The weeds wear moon mist mourning veils.
The weeds come high as six little crosses,
   One little cross for each couple.

CALIGARI

MANNIKINS, we command you.
Stand up with your white beautiful skulls.
Stand up with your moaning sockets.
Dance your stiff limping dances.
We handle you with spic and span gloves.
We tell you when and how
And how much.

FEATHER LIGHTS

MACABRE and golden the moon opened a slant of light.

A triangle for an oriole to stand and sing, " Take me home."

A layer of thin white gold feathers for a child queen of gypsies.

So the moon opened a slant of light and let it go.

So the lonesome dogs, the fog moon, the pearl mist, came back.

PEARL HORIZONS

UNDER a prairie fog moon
in a circle of pearl mist horizons,
a few lonesome dogs scraping thongs,
midnight is lonely; the fog moon midnight
takes up again its even smooth November.

Memories: you can flick me and sting me.
Memories, you can hold me even and smooth.

A circle of pearl mist horizons
is not a woman to be walked up to and kissed,
nor a child to be taken and held for a good-night,
nor any old coffee-drinking pal to be smiled at in
      the eyes and left with a grip and a handshake.

Pearl memories in the mist circling the horizon,
flick me, sting me, hold me even and smooth.

HOOF DUSK

THE dusk of this box wood
is leather gold, buckskin gold,
and the hoofs of a dusk goat
leave their heel marks on it.

The cover of this wooden box
is a last-of-the-sunset red,
a red with a sandman sand
fixed in evening siftings—
late evening sands are here.

The gold of old clocks,
forgotten in garrets,
hidden out between battles
of long wars and short wars,
the smoldering ember gold
of old clocks found again—
here is the small smoke fadeout
of their slow loitering.

Feel me with your fingers,
measure me in fire and wind:
maybe I am buckskin gold, old clock gold,
late evening sunset sand—

                    Let go
                    and loiter
                    in the smoke fadeout.

HARSK, HARSK

1

HARSK, harsk, the wind blows to-night.
What a night for a baby to come into the world!
What a night for a melodrama baby to come
    And the father wondering
    And the mother wondering
What the years will bring on their stork feet
Till a year when this very baby might be saying
On some storm night when a melodrama baby is born:
      " What a night
      for a baby
      to come into the world!! "
Harsk, harsk, the wind blows to-night.

2

It is five months off.
Knit, stitch, and hemstitch.
Sheets, bags, towels, these are the offerings.
When he is older—or she is a big girl—
There may be flowers or ribbons or money
For birthday offerings. Now, however,
We must remember it is a naked stranger
Coming to us, and the sheath of the arrival

Is so soft we must be ready, and soft too.
Knit, stitch, hemstitch, it is only five months.

3

It would be easy to pick a lucky star for this baby
If a choice of two stars lay before our eyes,
One a pearl gold star and one pearl silver,
And the offer of a chance to pick a lucky star.

4

When the high hour comes
Let there be a light flurry of snow,
A little zigzag of white spots
    Against the gray roofs.
The snow-born all understand this as a luck-wish.

BRANCUSI

BRANCUSI is a galoot; he saves tickets to take him no-where; a galoot with his baggage ready and no time table; ah yes, Brancusi is a galoot; he understands birds and skulls so well, he knows the hang of the hair of the coils and plaits on a woman's head, he knows them so far back he knows where they came from and where they are going; he is fathoming down for the secrets of the first and the oldest makers of shapes.

Let us speak with loose mouths to-day not at all about Brancusi because he has hardly started nor is hardly able to say the name of the place he wants to go when he has time and is ready to start; O Brancusi, keeping hardwood planks around your doorsteps in the sun waiting for the hardwood to be harder for your hard hands to handle, you Brancusi with your chisels and hammers, birds going to cones, skulls going to eggs—how the hope hugs your heart you will find one cone, one egg, so hard when the earth turns mist there among the last to go will be a cone, an egg.

Brancusi, you will not put a want ad in the papers telling God it will be to his advantage to come around and see you; you will not grow gabby and spill God earfuls of prayers; you will not get fresh and familiar as if God is a next-door neighbor and you have counted His shirts on a clothes line; you will go stammering, stuttering and mumbling or you will be silent as a mouse in a church garret when the pipe organ is pouring ocean waves on the sunlit rocks of ocean shores; if God is saving a corner for any battling bag of bones, there will be one for you, there will be one for you, Brancusi.

AMBASSADORS OF GRIEF

THERE was a little fliv of a woman loved one man and lost out. And she took up with another and it was a blank again. And she cried to God the whole layout was a fake and a frame-up. And when she took up with Number Three she found the fires burnt out, the love power, gone. And she wrote a letter to God and dropped it in a mail-box. The letter said:

O God, ain't there some way you can fix it up so the little flivs of women, ready to throw themselves in front of railroad trains for men they love, can have a chance? I guessed the wrong keys, I battered on the wrong panels, I picked the wrong roads. O God, ain't there no way to guess again and start all over back where I had the keys in my hands, back where the roads all came together and I had my pick?

And the letter went to Washington, D. C., dumped into a dump where all letters go addressed to God—and no house number.

WITHOUT THE CANE AND THE DERBY

(For C. C.)

THE woman had done him wrong.
Either that . . . or the woman was clean as a white rose
in the morning gauze of dew.
It was either one or the other or it was the two things,
right and wrong, woven together like two braids of
a woman's head of hair hanging down woven together.

The room is dark. The door opens. It is Charlie playing
for his friends after dinner, " the marvelous urchin,
the little genius of the screen," (chatter it like a
monkey's running laughter cry.)
No . . . it is not Charlie . . . it is somebody else. It
is a man, gray shirt, bandana, dark face. A candle
in his left hand throws a slant of light on the dark
face. The door closes slow. The right hand leaves
the door knob slow.

He looks at something. What is it? A white sheet on a
table. He takes two long soft steps. He runs the
candle light around a hump in the sheet. He lifts the
sheet slow, sad like.
A woman's head of hair shows, a woman's white face. He
takes the head between his hands and looks long at

it. His fingers trickle under the sheet, snap loose
something, bring out fingers full of a pearl necklace.
He covers the face and the head of hair with the white
sheet. He takes a step toward the door. The necklace
slips into his pocket off the fingers of his right hand.
His left hand lifts the candle for a good-by look.

Knock, knock, knock. A knocking the same as the time
of the human heartbeat.
Knock, knock, knock, first louder, then lower. Knock,
knock, knock, the same as the time of the human
heartbeat.
He sets the candle on the floor . . . leaps to the white
sheet . . . rips it back . . . has his fingers at the
neck, his thumbs at the throat, and does three slow
fierce motions of strangling.
The knocking stops. All is quiet. He covers the face and
the head of hair with the white sheet, steps back,
picks up the candle and listens.
Knock, knock, knock, a knocking the same as the time
of the human heartbeat.
Knock, knock, knock, first louder, then lower. Knock,
knock, knock, the same as the time of the human
heartbeat.
Again the candle to the floor, the leap, the slow fierce
motions of strangling, the cover-up of the face and
the head of hair, the step back, the listening.
And again the knock, knock, knock . . . louder . . .
lower . . . to the time of the human heartbeat.
Once more the motions of strangling . . .then . . .
nothing at all . . . nothing at all . . . no more

knocking . . . no knocking at all . . . no knocking
at all . . . in the time of the human heartbeat.

He stands at the door . . . peace, peace, peace everywhere only in the man's face so dark and his eyes
so lighted up with many lights, no peace at all, no
peace at all.

So he stands at the door, his right hand on the door knob,
the candle slants of light fall and flicker from his
face to the straight white sheet changing gray against
shadows.

So there is peace everywhere . . . no more knocking . . .
no knocking at all to the time of the human heartbeat . . . so he stands at the door and his right hand
on the door knob.

And there is peace everywhere . . . only the man's face
is a red gray plaster of storm in the center of peace
. . . so he stands with a candle at the door . . . so
he stands with a red gray face.

After he steps out the door closes; the door, the door
knob, the table, the white sheet, there is nothing at
all; the owners are shadows; the owners are gone;
not even a knocking; not even a knock, knock,
knock . . . louder, lower, in the time of the human
heartbeat.

The lights are snapped on. Charlie, " the marvelous
urchin, the little genius of the screen " (chatter it
with a running monkey's laughter cry) Charlie is
laughing a laugh the whole world knows.

The room is full of cream yellow lights. Charlie is
  laughing . . . louder . . . lower . . .
And again the heartbeats laugh . . . the human heartbeats laugh. . . .

THE RAKEOFF AND THE GETAWAY

" SHALL we come back? " the gamblers asked.
" If you want to, if you feel that way," the answer.

And they must have wanted to,
they must have felt that way;
for they came back,
hats pulled down over their eyes
as though the rain or the policemen
or the shadows of a sneaking scar-face Nemesis
followed their tracks and hunted them down.

" What was the clean-up? Let's see the rakeoff,"
somebody asked them, looking into their eyes
far under the pulled-down hat rims;
and their eyes had only the laugh of the rain in them,
lights of escape from a sneaking scar-face Nemesis
hunting their tracks, hunting them down.

Anvils, pincers, mosquitoes, anguish, raspberries,
steaks and gravy, remorse, ragtime, slang,
a woman's looking glass to be held in the hand
for looking at the face and the face make-up,
blackwing birds fitted onto slits
of the sunsets they were flying into,
bitter green waters, clear running waters,

standing pools ringing the changes
of all the triangles of the equinoxes of the sky,
  and a woman's slipper
  with a tarnished buckle,
  a tarnished Chinese silver buckle.

The gamblers snatched their hats off babbling,
" Some layout—take your pick, kid."

And their eyes had yet in them
the laugh of the rain
and the lights of their getaway
from a sneaking scar-face Nemesis.

TWO HUMPTIES

THEY tried to hand it to us on a platter,
Us hit in the eyes with marconigrams from moon
    dancers—
And the bubble busted, went flooey, on a thumb touch.

  So this time again, Humpty,
We cork our laughs behind solemn phizzogs,
Sweep the floor with the rim of our hats
And say good-a-by and good-a-by, just like that.

    To-morrow maybe they will be hit
    In the eyes with marconigrams
    From moon dancers.
Good-a-by, our hats and all of us say good-a-by.

IMPROVED FARM LAND

TALL timber stood here once, here on a corn belt farm
    along the Monon.

Here the roots of a half mile of trees dug their runners
    deep in the loam for a grip and a hold against wind
    storms.

Then the axmen came and the chips flew to the zing of
    steel and handle—the lank railsplitters cut the big
    ones first, the beeches and the oaks, then the brush.

Dynamite, wagons and horses took the stumps—the
    plows sunk their teeth in—now it is first class corn
    land—improved property—and the hogs grunt over
    the fodder crops.

It would come hard now for this half mile of improved
    farm land along the Monon corn belt, on a piece of
    Grand Prairie, to remember once it had a great
    singing family of trees.

HELL ON THE WABASH

WHEN country fiddlers held a convention in
Danville, the big money went to a barn dance
artist who played Turkey in the Straw, with
variations.

They asked him the name of the piece calling
it a humdinger and he answered, " I call it
' Hell On The Wabash.' "

The two next best were The Speckled Hen, and
Sweet Potatoes Grow in Sandy Land, with
variations.

THIS—FOR THE MOON—YES?

THIS is a good book?   Yes?
Throw it at the moon.
Stand on the ball of your right foot
And come to the lunge of a center fielder
Straddling in a throw for the home plate,
Let her go—spang—this book for the moon
    —yes?
And then—other books, good books, even the
    best books—shoot 'em with a long twist
    at the moon—yes?

PRIMER LESSON

Look out how you use proud words.
When you let proud words go, it is
    not easy to call them back.
They wear long boots, hard boots; they
    walk off proud; they can't hear you
    calling—
Look out how you use proud words.

SLABS OF THE SUNBURNT WEST

Meditation on Civilization

1

INTO the night, into the blanket of night,
Into the night rain gods, the night luck gods,
Overland goes the overland passenger train.

  Stand up, sandstone slabs of red,
Tell the overland passengers who burnt you.

Tell 'em how the jacks and screws loosened you.
Tell 'em who shook you by the heels and stood you on
     your heads,
Who put the slow pink of sunset mist on your faces.

Panels of the cold gray open night,
Gates of the Great American Desert,
    Skies keeping the prayers of the wagon men,
    The riders with picks, shovels and guns,
On the old trail, the Santa Fe trail, the Raton pass
Panels, skies, gates, listen to-night while we send up our
     prayers on the Santa Fe trail.

    (A colossal bastard frog
    squats in stone.
    Once he squawked.
    Then he was frozen and
    shut up forever.)

Into the night the overland passenger train,
Slabs of sandstone red sink to the sunset red,
Blankets of night cover 'em up.
Night rain gods, night luck gods, are looking on.

March on, processions.
Tie your hat to the saddle and ride, O Rider.
Let your ponies drag their navels in the sand.
Go hungry; leave your bones in the desert sand.
When the desert takes you the wind is clean.
The winds say so on a noisy night.

      The fingerbone of a man
      lay next to the handle of a frying pan
      and the footbone of a horse.
" Clean, we are clean," the winds whimper on a noisy
                                     night.

Into the night the overland passenger train,
And the engineer with an eye for signal lights,
And the porters making up berths for passengers,
And the boys in the diner locking the ice-box—
And six men with cigars in the buffet car mention
    " civilization," " history," " God."

Into the blanket of night goes the overland train,
Into the black of the night the processions march,
    The ghost of a pony goes by,
    A hat tied to the saddle,
    The wagon tongue of a prairie schooner
    And the handle of a Forty-niner's pickax

Do a shiver dance in the desert dust,
In the coyote gray of the alkali dust.
And—six men with cigars in the buffet car mention
   " civilization," " history," " God."

Sleep, O wonderful hungry people.
Take a shut-eye, take a long old snooze,
   and be good to yourselves;
Into the night the overland passenger train
And the sleepers cleared for a morning sun
   and the Grand Canyon of Arizona.

2   *Meditation on Glue*

A bluejay blue
and a gray mouse gray
ran up the canyon walls.

A rider came to the rim
Of a slash and a gap of desert dirt—
A long-legged long-headed rider
On a blunt and a blurry jackass—
Riding and asking, " How come? How come? "

And the long-legged long-headed rider said:
" Between two ears of a blurry jackass
I see ten miles of auburn, gold and purple—
I see doors open over doorsills
And always another door and a doorsill.
Cheat my eyes, fill me with the float
Of your dream, you auburn, gold, and purple.

Cheat me, blow me off my pins onto footless floors.
Let me put footsteps in an airpath.
Cheat me with footprints on auburn, gold, purple
Out to the last violet shimmer of the float
Of the dream—and I will come straddling a jackass,
Singing a song and letting out hallelujahs
To the door sill of the last footprint."

And the man took a stub lead pencil
And made a long memo in shorthand
On the two blurry jackass ears:—

" God sits with long whiskers in the sky."
I said it when I was a boy.
I said it because long-whiskered men
Put it in my head to say it.
          They lied . . . about you . . . God . . .
          They lied. . . .

The other side of the five doors
and doorsills put in my house—
how many hinges, panels, doorknobs,
how many locks and lintels,
put on the doors and doorsills
winding and wild between
the first and the last doorsill of all?

" Out of the footprints on ten miles
of auburn, gold and purple—an old song comes:
These bones shall rise again,
Yes, children, these bones shall rise.

" Yonder past my five doors
are fifty million doors, maybe,
stars with knobs and locks and lintels,
stars with riders of rockets,
stars with swimmers of fire.

" Cheat my eyes—and I come again—
straddling a jackass—singing a song—
letting out hallelujahs.

" If God is a proud and a cunning Bricklayer,
Or if God is a King in a white gold Heaven,
Or if God is a Boss and a Watchman always watching,
I come riding the old ride of the humiliation,
Straddling a jackass, singing a song,
Letting out hallelujahs.

" Before a ten mile float
of auburn, gold, and purple,
footprints on a sunset airpath haze,
     I ask:
How can I taste with my tongue a tongueless God?
How can I touch with my fingers a fingerless God?
How can I hear with my ears an earless God?
Or smell of a God gone noseless long ago?
Or look on a God who never needs eyes for looking?

" My head is under your foot, God.
My head is a pan of alkali dust
your foot kicked loose—your foot of air
with its steps on the sunset airpath haze.

(A bluejay blue
and a gray mouse gray
ran up the canyon walls.)

" Sitting at the rim of the big gap
at the high lash of the frozen storm line,
I ask why I go on five crutches,
tongues, ears, nostrils—all cripples—
eyes and nose—both cripples—
I ask why these five cripples
limp and squint and gag with me,
why they say with the oldest frozen faces:
        Man is a poor stick and a sad squirt;
        if he is poor he can't dress up;
        if he dresses up he don't know any place to go.

" Away and away on some green moon
a blind blue horse eats white grass
        And the blind blue horse knows more than I do
        because he saw more than I have seen
        and remembered it after he went blind.

" And away and away on some other green moon
is a sea-kept child who lacks a nose I got
and fingers like mine and all I have.
And yet the sea-kept child knows more than
I do and sings secrets alien to me as light
to a nosing mole underground.
I understand this child as a yellow-belly
catfish in China understands peach pickers
at sunrise in September in a Michigan orchard.

" The power and lift of the sea
and the flame of the old earth fires under,
I sift their meanings of sand in my fingers.
I send out five sleepwalkers to find out who I am,
    my name and number, where I came from,
    and where I am going.
They go out, look, listen, wonder, and shoot a fire-white
    rocket across the night sky; the shot and the flare
    of the rocket dies to a whisper; and the night is the
    same as it always was.
They come back, my five sleepwalkers; they have an
    answer for me, they say; they tell me: *Wait*—the
    password all of them heard when the fire-white rocket
    shot across the sky and died to a whisper, the pass-
    word is: *Wait*.

" I sit with five binoculars, amplifiers, spectroscopes
I sit looking through five windows, listening, tasting,
    smelling, touching.
I sit counting five million smoke fogs.
Repeaters, repeaters, come back to my window sills.
Some are pigeons coming to coo and coo and clean their
    tail feathers and look wise at me.
Some are pigeons coming with broken wings to die with
    pain in their eyes on my window sills.

" I walk the high lash of the frozen storm line;
I sit down with my feet in a ten-mile gravel pit.
Here I ask why I am a bag of sea-water fastened
to a frame of bones put walking on land—here I
look at crawlers, crimson, spiders spotted with

purple spots on their heads, flinging silver nets,
two, four, six, against the sun.
Here I look two miles down to the ditch of the sea
and pick a winding ribbon, a river eater, a water
grinder; it is a runner sent to run by a stop-watch,
it is a wrecker on a rush job."

     (A bluejay blue
     and a gray mouse gray
     ran up the canyon walls.)

Battering rams, blind mules, mounted policemen,
trucks hauling caverns of granite, elephants
grappling gorillas in a death strangle, cathedrals,
arenas, platforms, somersaults of telescoped railroad train wrecks, exhausted egg heads, piles of
skulls, mountains of empty sockets, mummies of kings
and mobs, memories of work gangs and wrecking crews,
sobs of wind and water storms, all frozen and held
on paths leading on to spirals of new zigzags—

An arm-chair for a one-eyed giant;
two pine trees grow in the left arm of the chair;
a bluejay comes, sits, goes, comes again;
a bluejay shoots and twitters . . out and across . .
tumbled skyscrapers and wrecked battleships,
walls of crucifixions and wedding breakfasts;
ruin, ruin—a brute gnashed, dug, kept on—
kept on and quit: and this is It.

Falling away, the brute is working.
Sheets of white veils cross a woman's face.
An eye socket glooms and wonders.
The brute hangs his head and drags on to the job.
The mother of mist and light and air murmurs: Wait.

The weavers of light weave best in red,
    better in blue.
The weavers of shadows weave at sunset;
    the young black-eyed women run, run, run
    to the night star homes; the old women
    sit weaving for the night rain gods,
    the night luck gods.

Eighteen old giants throw a red gold shadow ball;
they pass it along; hands go up and stop it; they
bat up flies and practice; they begin the game, they
knock it for home runs and two-baggers; the pitcher
put it across in an out- and an in-shoot drop; the
Devil is the Umpire; God is the Umpire; the game
is called on account of darkness.

    A bluejay blue
    and a gray mouse gray
    ran up the canyon walls.

Good night; it is scribbled on the panels
of the cold grey open desert.

Good night; on the big sky blanket over the
Santa Fe trail it is woven in the oldest
Indian blanket songs.

Buffers of land, breakers of sea, say it and
say it, over and over, good night, good night.

> Tie your hat to the saddle
> and ride, ride, ride, O Rider.
> Lay your rails and wires
> and ride, ride, ride, O Rider.

> The worn tired stars say
> you shall die early and die dirty.
> The clean cold stars say
> you shall die late and die clean.

> The runaway stars say
> you shall never die at all,
> never at all.